# THE ANTI-COOKING BIBLE

## 50 Ways To Get Out Of Cooking

### Written and illustrated by
### Maureen Ann Clarke

A Grackle Book

Grackle Publishing - Ambler, Pennsylvania

Grackle
An imprint of Grackle Publishing, LLC
gracklepublishing.com

Copyright © 2019 Maureen Ann Clarke
Illustration Copyright © 2019 Maureen Ann Clarke

All rights reserved.

ISBN: 978-0-9982069-9-8

The sound of the alarm blasts, *"MOM, WHAT'S FOR DINNER?"* Red alert! Panic rushes through me, my head spins and I start to sweat. The mere question stirs anxiety....

"What's in the fridge? Do I have to go shopping? What will they eat? How do I cook it? How do I get out of this? I hate cooking!"

–Maureen Ann Clarke

For Ed,
my love and my rock.

Because of you, I eat well and laugh a lot ...

... but not at the same time,
because that could get messy.

# Contents

| | |
|---|---|
| The Initiation | 7 |
| Avoidance | 16 |
| Dining Out | 23 |
| Re-Heating | 32 |
| No-Cook Meals | 35 |
| Unintentional Incidents | 39 |
| Hope For The Future | 44 |

*"How hard could it be?"*

–Maureen Ann Clarke

# The Initiation

My relationship with cooking started when I was a preteen. It was my father's birthday. Someone had to bake the cake. How hard could it be?

A tomboy at heart, I'd much rather play sports than spend time in the kitchen, but my mother insisted. She wanted to pass along her skills, so I followed her lead and set my inaugural cooking day on fire.

I decided on a boxed yellow cake with chocolate frosting. The directions seemed simple enough to follow. In no time at all, I carried the still warm cake into the dining room, candles ablaze. I was so proud as we sang the ritual birthday song.

The cake *looked* delicious.

As master chef, I had the honor of cutting the cake. Everyone waited for me to serve the last slice before digging in. Then, without warning, each and every person gagged and spat out their bite in disgust!

My first foray into the realm of "culinary delight" and my cake made everyone spit violently with sound effects to boot!

I looked at my family in horror. I ran from the room crying and embarrassed. I was done. Gone. Bye-bye. My epic fail scarred me for life ... at my grand ol' age of twelve!

Would I ever learn how to cook?

**spit** *verb*
spit or spat; spitting

to show contempt by ejecting something from the mouth, often with explosive sound.

After my eventual return from my bedroom, my mother reviewed the ingredients of the cake with me. As we dissected the list, we found two problems:

1. I had used margarine instead of butter. Not the end of the world, but...

2. Margarine was an especially bad choice to use in combination with the rancid shortening used to grease the pan.

Well, how the heck would I know the shortening was spoiled?!!

It was on the shelf, ready to go. Sure, it smelled weird, but as far as I knew, that was normal for vegetable shortening.

How many twelve-year-olds check expiration dates or know how to sniff out a bad ingredient?

It was a year later before I dared step back into the kitchen. I was a teenager now and a bit braver at thirteen. I craved soft-boiled eggs, so I put the eggs in the warming water.

Then I remembered how my mother used to say, "A watched pot never boils." So I sat down in the living room and watched the television instead. It would only take a few minutes for my eggs to cook.

As teenagers can sometimes get distracted, I found myself engrossed in whatever half-hour show was on. Toward the end of the program, I heard a loud noise in the kitchen. The kitchen? The eggs!

I raced into the kitchen with my arms covering my face as the pot burst into flames. Egg grenades were exploding everywhere, shooting out of the pot, hitting me and the ceiling!

When the fire company got involved, my family thought it would be funny to display HAZMAT labels.

Though the warning signs that were posted urged love, not war, my family fired regular reminders of the grenade egg story at me for decades. Their recounts packed a lot of fire power and kept me far from the kitchen.

Ten years later, at twenty-three, I got married.

I wanted to cook for my husband. Seriously, I did. I started with traditional meals and experimented with new ones. But I soon discovered my bridegroom to be the pickiest eater on the planet!

He wanted baked chicken with no spices at all, tomato sauce with no garlic, oregano, onions or spices. Everything had to be bland. He disliked ethnic foods. So, no Mexican, Chinese, kielbasa and sauerkraut (my German roots), or even mashed potatoes. Really?!!

Baked chicken, roast beef, plain baked potato, French fries, broccoli, ham, salads with just lettuce, plain pizza, and plain cheese steaks (we're from Philly) were the basis of our menu. This did not help me overcome my disinterest in cooking or heal my damaged ego from those youthful mishaps.

With all this stifling my creativity, I thought, "What's next?"

I shouldn't have asked.

My husband told me that he liked my mother's lasagna. So I wanted to surprise him with a special birthday dinner. I had never made a lasagna. How hard could it be?

The recipe called for a few different cheeses, sauce, and lasagna noodles. Seemed simple enough. I threw it together, baked it, and we ate it.

It tasted surprisingly good.

Then a few hours later … BAM! We end up in the emergency room. My spouse suffered from intense pain and cramping in his abdomen.

I vowed to never cook again.

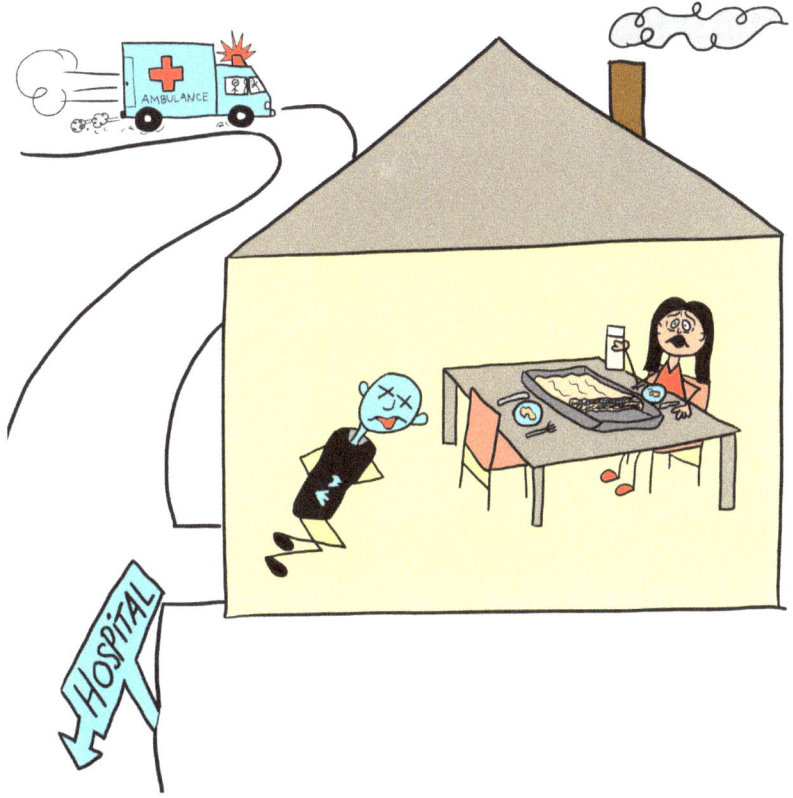

"Gastroenteritis."

Gastroenteritis was the big term the doctor used to describe his diagnosis: irritation and inflammation of the stomach and intestines.

## Rx

The doctor said certain foods may irritate the stomach and cause this condition. Lactose intolerance to dairy products was a possible cause in this situation. I put too much cheese into one meal. Another nail in the cooking coffin!

## Résumé

By the age of twenty-three, my cooking resume boasted of a spoiled birthday cake, grenade eggs with a side of fire, and a poisonous lasagna.

## Pièce de Résistance

Now with an additional twenty-five years of burning meals, raising two picky children and surviving a divorce, I present to you my masterpiece, *The Anti-Cooking Bible: 50 Ways To Get Out of Cooking*.

If you too cringe at the thought of cooking, I hope this guide will help you find some practical tips.

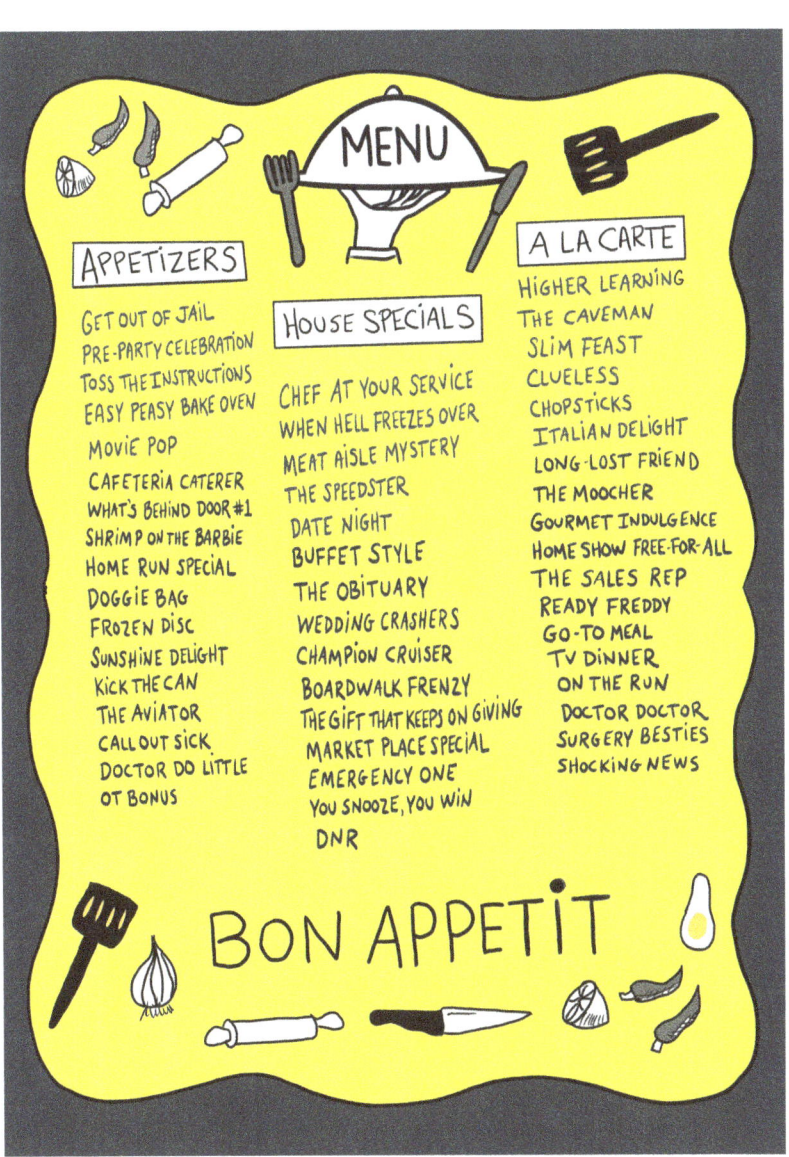

**50 Ways To Get Out Of Cooking**

## **Avoidance**

Every time my mother called for me to watch her cook, I would find a way to slip out the door. At an early age, "Gotta go to the bathroom," "I don't feel so good" and "I have to do homework" were my favorite excuses. Now, as a master of the art of avoidance, I begin *50 Ways To Get Out Of Cooking* with these go-to tips.

**Chef at Your Service**

If I could afford a personal chef, the book would end here! However, since I don't have a money tree in my yard, I must take on the dreaded evil task myself—or choose one of the next forty-nine excuses to wriggle my way out.

**Get Out of Jail**

When your significant other goes above and beyond and delivers you breakfast in bed, reward him or her with a "get out of jail" card to use later if and when trouble breaks out.

Exchanging such a card can keep humor in a relationship and stop petty arguments from spiraling out of control.

When my partner pulls out that card, I am immediately reminded of the wonderful person he is and all he does for me!

### Pre-Party Celebration

Go early to a special event, like a "cake and ice cream only" birthday party. In our family, we celebrate birthdays by having family over after dinner, serving hors d'oeuvres and cake and ice cream. This is an opportunity to fill up on these mini meals and dessert and skip cooking dinner.

### Higher Learning

Go back to college or attend night school or a class. This may seem like a drastic measure to avoid cooking, but it kills two birds with one stone. You receive an education, increasing your likelihood of a better income, while dodging the deed at the same time. A win-win situation right there!

# #5 The Caveman

Designate grilling nights. Around here, the cave men of the family do most (if not all) of the grilling. Burgers, hot dogs, chicken and fish on the grill are all tasty dinners.

# Slim Feast #6

Go on a diet. Although you shouldn't skip meals when you are dieting, we all know that we do this once in a while. Instead, make a meal replacement shake, which packs a lot of nutrition and fills you up until the next meal. Throw in some fruit and leafy greens, and you have yourself an entire meal in a cup. Sustenance at its finest!

## #7 Toss the Instructions

Never read a recipe. This is like tossing out the instructions before putting together a cabinet or bicycle. Who needs instructions or a recipe? Just throw together some ingredients and it will be close enough, right? WRONG! And hopefully, if it tastes bad, they won't ask you to cook again.

## #8 Clueless

Being totally clueless has its rewards. If you have no clue what food you have in stock or how to cook it, then it's much easier to make last-minute meal decisions such as dining out or quick, no-cook meals.

### When Hell Freezes Over ... # 9

I might get around to cooking! Somewhere in the depths of my subconscious mind, I believe if I put off defrosting that chicken, maybe someone else will end up cooking it. Why is all our food freezer-burned? The devil must have zapped it!

### Easy Peasy Bake Oven # 10

Sign up the kids for a cooking class. For me, this would have two obvious benefits: the kids learn something I could not teach, and they can practice their new cooking skills whenever they want. Hey, I'm not picky—I'll eat just about anything!

**Meat Aisle Mystery**

Grocery stores are AAA-grade, if not prime mazes. It's best to get in and out quickly—and it's especially important to avoid the meat aisle (there's a meat aisle?).

You could spend all your valuable time choosing meats or other main courses for the week, but remember the unwritten rule: "He who buys it, cooks it."

# Dining Out

If I fail at avoidance, I will consult my list of dining out categories, which includes: favorite restaurants, other go-to establishments, homes owned by others, and finally, anyone who delivers.

Often, it ends up being a "fend for yourself" dinner. My kids will need to use each and every suggestion in this book to find a way to feed themselves. I feel being capable of "fending for yourself" is a valuable skill for all children to grasp. After all, if my children ever get lost in the wilderness, they will be equipped with the skills necessary to survive on their own.

## #12 The Speedster

Get takeout from a fast-food restaurant chain. In our neck of the woods, Chick fil-A is a healthier fast-food option compared to some other fast-food establishments. They have grilled chicken nuggets, and their waffle fries are an enticing alternative to standard fries. A grilled chicken salad can make you feel less guilty about ordering out.

## Chopsticks #13

Chinese food night. Chinese food is a tasty treat, and is often the only time my children eat their vegetables! I do not consider Chinese food fast-food, although they usually have it ready in "10 minutes" no matter how busy they are.

## #14 Italian Delight

Pizza night. Who doesn't love pizza night? Pick your favorite pizza place and surprise the kids. Delivery every Friday works for me!

### Date Night

I love going out for dinner. Whenever I hear "would you like to," I'll interrupt with "yes, of course!" My partner will laugh, wondering how I knew what he was going to say. Believe me, I know when I'm being asked out for dinner. And he knows I'll jump at the chance to get out of cooking.

 ### Movie Pop

Go to the movies late in the afternoon and get an extra-large bucket of popcorn. Not only will you be full, but you will have successfully dined out and avoided cooking.

### Buffet Style

Go to all-you-can-eat buffets. Fill up on as much as you can eat, then take leftovers home so you have a meal for the next day.

# #18 Long-Lost Friend

Call a friend you haven't seen in six months and make plans to go out to dinner. The benefits are many: you connect with a friend you haven't seen in a while, you avoid cooking that night, and you get a good meal.

# #19 The Obituary

Attend as many funerals as possible. I know this sounds distasteful, even morbid, to take advantage of an unfortunate circumstance, but as we get older, such opportunities are inevitable. People drop like flies. We must pay our respects to their families. So stick around till the end, the family may invite the attendees to a post-service gathering. Sometimes these are the best meals and turn out to be wonderful impromptu family reunions.

### Cafeteria Caterer

Visit a friend in the hospital and eat in the cafeteria. Visiting people in the hospital not only benefits the sick person, but you can enjoy having a decent meal in the cafeteria and check off another box on the get-out-of-cooking list. Well done!

### Wedding Crashers

Crash a wedding. OK, I have never done this, but it is on my bucket list. I have heard of couples who do this to test out the caterer before deciding on one for their own wedding. Go ahead, go all Vince Vaughn and Owen Wilson at the next reception. Just keep in mind you can get arrested for this (I've heard).

 **The Moocher**

Visit your mother—yes, the one who tried to teach you to cook. She's good at cooking, so why not mooch a meal from her? Besides, what mom doesn't love a visit from her kids, and she will always cook for them no matter how old they are! This we can count on, especially if your mom is Italian! I'm not Italian, but I lined myself up with an Italian friend so I can visit her mom and get a great dinner. Now I get a meal from my mom, and another from my friend's mom. Don't forget to take your kids too!

**Champion Cruiser**

All-inclusive vacationing. If you can afford to go on a vacation, a great option is an all-inclusive cruise. This allows you one week of the year to skip the task of cooking, while looking like a real champ to the kids for taking them on a cruise!

# #24

### What's Behind Door #1

Get a part-time job as a food demonstrator. You can sample the food you put out, even if it's only potato chips. By the end of the night, your tummy will be full and you won't be in the mood to eat dinner. If you are lucky, you will be presenting the new meatballs which have just hit the shelves!

### Gourmet Indulgence

Go to all-you-can-eat dinners. Usually churches or VFWs hold Sunday all-you-can-eat spaghetti night or something similar. By doing this, you are helping to support the community while getting out of cooking. Win-win!

### Shrimp on the Barbie

Attend any and all barbecues. While these opportunities usually happen more in the summer, it's best to plan your "get out of cooking" nights on a regular basis throughout the year. Seriously, any warm night will do!

 **Home Run Special**

Eat at the snack stand at kids' sporting events. Your kids will love it and you'll get out of cooking for the night. Even if the home team loses ... you still win!

 **Home Show Free-for-All**

Attend home shows with food tastings. Most home shows have food tastings at every other table. Just walk the aisles a few times and you will eat enough to satisfy dinner!

# #29

### Boardwalk Frenzy

Eat at the boardwalk while on vacation. I consider anything dinner while we are at the "boards." Cheese fries, pizza, ice cream—all qualify as dinner!

# Reheating

Some easy-to-heat meals are waiting for you in your refrigerator or at your grocery store. So take care to shop wisely and remember to save your leftovers—or as my mother put it, "Don't waste food; there are starving people in the world." She meant well—and more importantly, I learned that leftovers one night meant a meal for the next day. Here are a few suggestions that will get you through the week.

### The Sales Rep  #30

Bring home leftovers from work parties and sales representatives. I work at a hospital and we frequently have sales reps who supply lunch for the employees. They bring enough to feed an army, so there's always leftover food. Pack plenty to go and, hey, mama's got dinner!

### Doggie Bag

Bring home a "doggie bag" from every party you attend. Other people's parties are great because that is dinner for two nights! If the host is a relative, odds are they will ask if you want to take food home. Your answer should always be yes!

### The Gift That Keeps on Giving

Leftovers from big holidays like Christmas, Rosh Hashanah, Easter, etc., usually offer the opportunity for tons of leftovers. These make awesome dinners for the entire week following the holiday, so plan accordingly!

### Frozen Disc

Frozen pizza. How easy can it get! Just heat and serve. You can even doctor it up with some added sauce, cheese or other tasty toppings. Keep a few of these staples in your freezer for a last-minute meal.

**Ready Freddy**

Get a hot, ready-to-eat rotisserie chicken at a major grocery store. They are a delicious, inexpensive option, and you can easily throw some bagged salad in a bowl to make a complete and healthy meal.

## No-cook Meals

*"Boiling water and heating sauce is easy and requires little to no thinking."*

—Maureen Ann Clarke

If I absolutely must cook, I'll check my list of quick or no-cook meals. Though some of these meals may technically be cooking, they are elementary and require limited cooking time. Whether you are a single-parent, working full-time and doing all you can stay afloat, a busy professional, or solo cook, this list will be indispensable. And when exhaustion has set in, these meals will be your salvation!

**Kick the Can**

Canned soup. Soups are a great option for their convenience and variety. All you have to do is throw them in a pot and heat for a few minutes. Include buttered bread or toast to balance your plate. Be careful not to burn your mouth on the soup as that would ruin your meal!

**Go-to Meal**

Pasta night. Boiling water and heating sauce is easy and requires little to no thinking. Always have pasta and a jar of tomato or clam sauce on your shelf. If you are exhausted after coming home from work and just don't want to think, this is the go-to meal!

**Sunshine Delight**

Breakfast for dinner. Cereal, toast, eggs, omelets, pancakes and waffles are all awesome dinners and, to me, really doesn't qualify as cooking. If you can make them while you are half asleep in the morning, then making them for dinner should be a piece of cake!

## TV Dinner

Microwave meals. This is an obvious choice for this category. Make sure you follow the instructions and don't over-heat or it will turn into tire rubber. Plant yourself in front of the TV and switch on your favorite show.

## Market Place Special

Sandwiches for dinner. Peanut butter and jelly, ham and cheese, roast beef, steak, tuna, egg or chicken salad, Italian or turkey hoagies are all delicious and convenient. Add a little side dish of fruit and you will have a quick and healthy meal.

**The Aviator**

Salads for dinner. Add your savory leftovers to a simple bag of greens to create a meal all its own. Grilled chicken Caesar salad, Cobb salad, etc., make for lite healthy meals. No leftovers, no problem! If you are on the fly, stop by the grocery store and pick up packaged cooked grilled chicken, hard boiled eggs, or shrimp to add to your salad.

**On the Run**

Sliced fruit, cheese and crackers, yogurt. These are light, but easy meals if you are counting calories or have a hectic, on-the-go lifestyle.

# Unintentional Incidents

The excuses in this category mimic avoidance. The main difference is they are (initially) unintentional. "What seems to us as bitter trials are often blessings in disguise." Growing up in Catholic school, we heard this phrase from Oscar Wilde a lot! Through the years, I would see the benefit of these uncannily timed and unfortunate incidents. How can I help it if I end up not being able to cook?

### Call Out Sick   #42

Call the boss (your kids), because being sick gets you out of cooking every time! The kitchen is no place for germs, that's for sure!

# #43 Doctor Doctor

To avoid using up your sick time for a doctor's appointment, schedule it at the end of the workday. I finish at 5 p.m., which is the typical dinnertime hour. I'm not able to be home to cook, so luckily, my significant other offers to cook for the kids.

# #44 Doctor Do Little

Might as well schedule that vet appointment after work too. Wow, what a guy! He volunteered to cook dinner for the kids again while I take the dogs to the vet! See a pattern here? My wonderful chef hero comes to the rescue again. I know, I'm lucky—and he's all mine!

# #45 Emergency One

Visit the emergency room. Seriously, not on purpose! This is just a coincidence that conveniently happens around dinnertime. Incidents like my son running into a tree or breaking his ankle on a trampoline offer opportunities for quality time and fine dining at the hospital cafeteria.

 **Surgery Besties**

Plan that needed surgery. If you are a full-glass kind of person, which I am, you'll see an important benefit of having that needed surgery. You find out who your best friends are—the ones who bring you dinner while you are recovering! Ten days of mandatory rest always works for me! Thank you, besties!

# 47 **OT Bonus**

Work overtime. This is my least favorite excuse, but sometimes you just have to put in extra time at work. Sure, you get paid the extra cash, but the real bonus is not having to cook that night.

### #48  You Snooze, You Win

Exhausted from a hard day's work (and the OT), you lie down for a few minutes. Upon awakening you realize that you have slept right through the dinner hour. Is there still time to cook? No need, everyone else has already eaten!

### #49  Shocking News

Power outage. These can happen without notice, and when they do, no one can cook! You can either throw together cold sandwiches ... or drive to another town with a restaurant that still has power. Let the others decide. Either way, you will get out of cooking again!

# #50  DNR (Do Not Resuscitate)

When the oven breaks, put off calling the repair service as long as you can. Obviously, you can't cook if your oven doesn't work. Aw shucks, it's dead, done, kaput. You hear "Taps" playing in the distance.

Maybe this is a sign. Maybe some of us were just not meant to cook.

## Hope For The Future

In an era of smart machines, there are robotic solutions for all kinds of tasks. Cars can drive without human intervention. Robots can perform surgery. Maybe in the future, there will be mainstream robots to do all our meal preparation, cooking and cleaning up!

There is hope! In 2015, a London-based robotics firm created a sophisticated robot that could cook 2,000 different meals. That solution was estimated to cost $10,000 to $15,000.

So, start saving your pennies, because this is one robot we all would welcome into our homes! Look out, George Jetson!

**Bon Appétit**

I hope you found some useful excuses, as they have served me well. Now, go on and get out of the kitchen, before someone sees you in there and asks, "What's for dinner?"

**By the way, would you like to buy a cookbook?**

A Grackle Book

www.ingramcontent.com/pod-product-compliance
Lightning Source LLC
Chambersburg PA
CBHW051554010526
44118CB00022B/2704